Making a Map of the River

Making a Map of the River

Poems and an Essay

Thorpe Moeckel

Iris Press
Oak Ridge, Tennessee

Iris Press is an imprint of the Iris Publishing Group, Inc.
www.irisbooks.com

Library of Congress Cataloging-in-Publication Data

Moeckel, Thorpe.
  Making a map of the river : poems / Thorpe Moeckel.
    p. cm.
  ISBN 978-1-60454-200-4 (hardcover : alk. paper)
  ISBN 978-1-60454-201-1 (pbk. : alk. paper)
  1. White-water canoeing—Poetry.
  2. Chattooga River (N.C.-Ga. and S.C.)—Poetry. I. Title.
PS3613.O334M35 2008
811'.6—dc22

                    2007050979

ACKNOWLEDGMENTS

Thanks to the editors of the following publications in whose pages some of these writings first appeared, sometimes in slightly different form: *Appalachian Heritage, Brighthouse, Poet Lore, Nantahala, storySouth, The Virginia Quarterly Review, Rivendell, Shenandoah, Tarpaulin Sky, Pisgah Review, Open City, Hotel Amerika, The Sow's Ear Poetry Review,* and *Wild Earth.*

The author would also like to thank Aaron Baker, Peter Relic, Kirsten, Sophie, Josef Beery, George Garrett, the Moeckel family, the Griffiths family, and John Lane for support and help with the poems. Thanks to UVA for a Henry Hoyns Fellowship, to UNC Chapel Hill for a Kenan Visiting Writer Position, and to Hollins University — the good times and good people at these places helped these poems to life.

The author wishes to thank The Chattooga Conservancy, a clean, wild tributary, by urging readers to visit and support them at www.chattoogariver.org.

For the Five Hole Gang

Suddenly the canoe was caught in the vortex, and the men were thrown out and sucked under the water.

A huge fish seized one of the men, and he was never heard of again. The other man was flung around and around and down and down until he came to the bottom of the whirlpool. Then another swirling circle caught him and brought him up to the surface. He floated to shallow water and managed to crawl ashore.

Afterward the man told about his experience:

When I was sucked down at the smallest circle of the whirlpool, the water seemed to open up below me. I could look down as through the roof beams of a house. On the bottom of the river I saw a great company of people. They looked up and beckoned me to join them. As they raised their hands to grab me another whirl of water caught me and carried me up out of reach.

—from Cherokee myth

CONTENTS

I — BRIDGE TO WOODALL

II — HIGH WATER

I

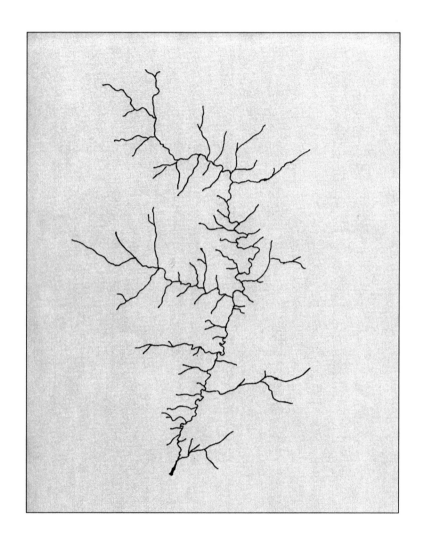

BRIDGE TO WOODALL

Night Walk

Maybe the eyes are only just at night, if they can be just at all

when open. Maybe everything seen is seen again, but not now.
  Now, what's fixed moves, and what moves
isn't there. Now, as trees sliver in their roots, the limbs

dispense another remedy for shallow breathing. Far off
  there's barking, and then it's gone but there

as when a sharp pain in the chest subsides, or the land & the sky
trade places. It's clear that dirt is blood's remix, that there
  is space available, so many square feet,

but whether the smilax & chokecherry wire some divinity,

whether the wires escape their conduit, like bedhead, or a visual
of the kingfisher's manic chatter, is less clear. The dark's weird;

  to say the pokeweed berries grow wiser,
for instance, or that the elm becomes a segment of Solid Gold,
  each limb a toll way of throb & sway

where memory is the DJ, spinning the vinyl of what comes next,
  is so much thanksgiving traffic.
   But here we are

  watching the moon's humors dilate
with each passing cloud, watching the mountain laurel do its best
  to be bamboo.

Bridge to Woodall

There must be a thousand eddies on the Chattooga River
between the bridge and Woodall Shoals, and after work
when the trips we guided were soggy memories, we'd catch

all of them, launch every angled, sloping ledge—frontwards,
backwards, edgewards, upside-downwards; we'd surf each wave,
from the least dimple to the pulsing monsters that formed

at highwater, when the Chattooga's amaretto ran whitecapped
and fast, eroding banks, tossing deadfall as if carrots
in a giant's mouth. Fiends for breathing that galax-pungent

escarpment air, we'd put on with haste, always ferrying
across to the South Carolina side, first, to check the gauge,
and then do a couple of rolls, a couple of pivot turns

if the boat was low volume, making sure the skirt fit right,
that it wouldn't pop on the first ender at Surfing Rapid.
Sometimes there'd be old timers in the shallows, turning

over rocks for jackdogs—catfish bait—& they'd look at us
the way shopkeepers look at skateboarders who are surfing
the sidewalk in front of their store—techno weenies

no matter how hard we tried to be retro, in our snazzy
lifevests, our pink brain buckets. A curious hunger
drove our play—part obsession, part adrenaline,

part longing to connect with gravity, time, water,
earth; but mostly each other, ourselves. There was
no garbage down there, no roads and no homes,

only lines, new & old, and depending on the water level
and what sort of boat you wore, and how long you'd been
wearing it, & some coefficient between where you wanted

it to go and how well you visualized it getting there, you were
on line, or off; at Surfing Rapid, S-Turn, Highwater Hole;
at Rock Jumble, Woodall, Screaming Left Hand Turn; lines,

eddy hops, elevator moves, backferries into sidesurfs,
screw ups, three sixties, pirouettes. "Hey, follow me,"
one of us always said, already getting momentum,

ninjastroking the little plastic casket, about to slice
into the meat of some frothing curler, uniform pourover,
or tripped out creekslot; and we did, we followed.

FLUSH

Pebbles & sand,
little loaves, pizza stones,
crust.

Isoclinal recumbent folds.
Ah, science.
Redeyes darting

into darker holes,
everything elephantine, fleshy,
cochleal. Mist

like the river's double, the hemlocks'
various shades
of shade. Mud between

the toes. What gospel
in the laurel siding,
in the red leaves

sunk to the bottom
where the beginning lives.
Maybe gradient

is wisdom's meow, is
grief's worst tenant.
Something. Seep-slap,

paste of rain-wet,
fall-soft leaves. Sticks
on the bank, sticks on the bank.

To read water
study a burl. Tsa-tugi
is God's sprinkler,

they say. Sandpiper, pileated,
husk. Old log
stuck tip first. Foam.

Spiderweb in spicebush.
Fish scales
of mica. Cinnamon ferns.

Eddy here. Hear
the wave's foliage.
Osprey. Phlox.

CROSS-FORWARD

By definition, a cross stroke occurs whenever canoeists move the paddle from their original paddling side across the boat's centerline to the opposite side of the canoe. The paddler does not switch his grip on the paddle; his hands remain in the same position.

—A.C.A.*Canoeing and Kayaking Instruction Manual*

I am a risk
and a naked-side. How unnatural
I feel at first,
how I tweak your shoulder.

Of course your body
is capable; without me,
you are destitute,
you are blind.

To know me—my mercy—you have to be bold,
vulnerable, fluent
in your faith,

and numb to nothing.

The obsession your boat needs,
the crisis—
I am less for pleasure
than to stand time on its head.

Use me in a sequence, fused with a few quick
on-sides, use me

like music on the lips of the river.

OUTWATER

Olivewhite with morning sun, the river
is ribbon candy.
                Sit down, it says.
Among bloodstone.
See in seep's mud, where black bear stepped.
Listen to the jewelweed
as it hums an orange grace.

*

It's bugthirst & big trees—
basswood, poplar, oak. It's burls
like gargoyles. And maybe despair once rooted here.
How else the wind bearing news
                       of the gorge,
its breakier reaches:
millipedes, cascades, trillium gone to fruit.

*

Pulse, maybe, or maybe
                body, how bulbs
of rhododendron blossoms begin
to open. Look here, under the laurel's last snow,
where softness grows softer:
furtherings—
seed of the lily, seed of the breeze.

*

Now the canopy bleeds
evening. Light like vastness puddles.
Updraft,
     where deadfall crocodiles
and bark slows to the scripture of being,
time's toadlike—it breathes you,
it pours you out.

*

Whatever bugs in sun say with their glide,
there's branchwork—knoll, confluence, nest—
in every breath, a limb,
a lambency, and maybe blossoms
still tremor in creekwind,
that stuff of collisions,
               of outwater, in.

*

Rootgrasp. Curve & nook. See
the bark's fretwork. Things bulbous,
flayed. Yes,
               the leaves weather.
Yes, drainage goddess licks them up.
Call it a whorled.
Spell it as you like.

*

Laddersplash, waves
in wrungs. Here giving means
letting in.
Consider the sieve,
                    peeled log hung
in nape. All the bughover.
Thrushthroat liquid & trill.

*

So the other world is this, the one
one slows to know.
            Nothing new. No
hurry in the stones. No gongs in the trees—
all's trance, all's shiver.
And in the stalks—their slightness,
their give.

IN THE RAFT BARN

I'd wake to the blowers or wake before,
then wake others when hitting the switch,
holding spout to valve, bent, knees on rubber.

Up there were runs in the plywood floor,
places where a layer'd flaked, where the glue
or whatever holds those sandwiches

together, had come loose, been scraped
or something, and I'm surprised none
of the rafts splintered a leak. Sure,

they were tough, built for bearing loads
on gneiss, schist, being tossed on bus roofs,
ratcheted in stacks. I saw one pop in the sun.

It wasn't anything dramatic, and we patched
the slit with toluene and rubber cement, got
that vehicle back in the water. The Chattooga

isn't fit for self-bailers or rafts too rockered;
these rafts were like Novas, heavy, ugly, tiring
to handle. But they tracked well. They took hits

and drops like hope, messy, which we liked,
because the Chattooga when low is a smash-up;
minefields & chutes: many needles to thread.

Squeal Like a Pig

some guest would always holler
on the bus, or in the parking lot
before getting close to the river,
and I'd turn, half expecting Dickey come barreling up—
dirty grin, hemorrhoidal gait. It's not
my favorite line of his, but I love him
for that scene & all his elegant, bestial pomp,
how the world turns meaty & vegetal
in his lens, like galax or the light
of a Winnebago on I-85
with *Deliverance* on the VCR & six drunks
yelling *let's go rafting*
as if they already weren't.

Below Warwoman Creek

Night, October. Bugsounds—crickets, katydid. Wood sizzles
like radiant vapor, shushes as it breaks.   Perhaps a river,
        too, burns—rocks as flint, water as steel.
                Above is a hemlock, next to it an oak, leaf-
thin with fall. As twilight fades, the dark illumines more stars—
agents of illusion, agents of the real—time they are,
                distant fires.

BIOPHONY

Laden, the poplar, and a bend
like limbo, like reaching
for a penny. For luck. Laden,

the foliage, Bondoing. In leaps
& shrouds. Say milk thistle,

propogule. Might blossoms
be songbooks? For hours
mythlings in bark slats toot &

holler leaky never nevers.
These chants of monkshood,

these kickbacks too camouflage
for reentry, the way damselfly
never lands the same way once.

How they surround is how
they carry. Really, bursts have

more room than voice. Fryolator,
seed-spit. Some forty grit
tears up the sun now. On a run.

By flicks, by zips. The cochlea,
the phonic, the barb. Heard

hoofprints. The blood heavy
& needing let. Yes, to sharpen
the comb on the flesh, wetten it,

press—surely belief forages
from the tongues it speaks.

Far Rain

The sun, a pumpkin in the August haze, oozed
on our guests as they bumped down a minty tongue
near the bank then were slammed deep by a hydraulic,

an activity we did only when the water was low.
Who was it noticed the rafts come unbeached, the first
blushings of silt? It hadn't rained in two weeks & a day,

and wasn't raining now, as far as we knew.
But who knows about the places where rocks are born,
the places where water rises & the river begins?

Was it the East Fork or the West whose driftwood
moseyed past? How many inches fell, how fast,
I wondered, roping in the swimmers, fetching

the raft, loading it, falling in line between
lead boat & sweep, picturing some great hole—
water from Kansas, salt water, no rain at all.

Middle Fall

It was a reunion. It was holy differently again.

I would not find
such unbarren society,
such theater of revere.

The kingfisher in its pale-collared habit
had fewer places to hide

and flew wildly,
dodging leaves no longer there.

What was eaten
was spared. Exposure, delight's face, faced

the interior out.
Flight made no bones

about magnificence. If the warbler
in vinesnag flaunted

its gift, why not
get down a little now & then,

really shake a wing.
The river does it forever.

Lifejackets

If as baby's bibs on the four old growth
NFL linemen in my raft, the lifejackets
were like bloated articles of faith
on the Baptist youth group
who'd fifteen-passengered up

from Pascagoula all night singing
Our God is an awesome God
he reigns from heaven above.
And if there was something of Houdini
in how the edgy, rose-nosed folks

from the strip joint wore them,
the executive looked as though
he'd cinched one on for years,
bound and so buoyant above
the depths, he couldn't see

to swim. For the grocer from Greenville
with a pill bottle of nitroglycerine
duct-taped to his guide's river shorts,
it was a straitjacket clamming
his courage like a fist, and, yes, from

the start the perfumists were aghast
at the stench — mildew, sweat-soup —
and discussed how to distill it, render
a base. But I tell you nobody wore
that Type Five P.F.D. as stylishly

as the pecan farmer, thumbs tucked
to arm-slits as though anything
he wore would be comfortable
since tropical winds leveled his farm
last August. *What did Hurricane Hugo*

say to the pecan tree, he asked the crew,
voice like leaves raised from the ground
by a gust, then settling. *You better*
hold on to your nuts, he said.
This ain't goin be no ordinary blowjob.

Song

Hepatica, bloodroot, wild geranium, violet.

*

Green tongues of sun & sheen —
it is their reach
like chopper blades, like spires.

*

There is no air like this on earth.

*

Aromas the color of water beneath
a shadow-hatched ledge.

*

The burst & boil. The
arcing V of diagonals.
Fansquirm. Drenched moss
and curl. Bubbles.
The brown, the browns.
Overmuch, mulched
over spindles
of wash. Has the lichen
farted? Giddy ions,
their gas.

*

Little caravans of stick & spit,
delicate as nose hair their trails in the silt.

*

It is their reach

✻

that tacks the o
            on gust,
the erotic
        into ecology.

✻

Plummet & boil, how
it goes birch, goes tin
and can, & does —
call it gravity's will,
a terrace
of curtain,
certain with splendor,
& fall.

Living There, Not Living There

Once you swam on New Year's Day,
not for long but your whole body was down
where the water is no longer green
and hugs you mighty hard. Another time,
near Three Forks, you watched a black snake
climb a black oak, then enter a hole,

all six feet of it, except the bait of the nub
of its tail. Were monarchs, cider bugs,
and walking sticks. And drowned things:
the fawn, the horse, the feral hog.
Why don't you live there anymore?
Because you do & don't even have to?

Because there's a stillhouse in your hollow
and a kingfisher screeching behind your eyes
each day whether you like it or not?
Or because you believe a bird came
to the black snake's tail, thinking it was
a beetle, thinking it was food.

ALL FORWARD, ALL BACK

The river is two-faced, the river is memory
and memory is forgetting. "All forward, all back,"
I yell to the mix of chefs & nurses in my raft,
who I don't see, who might not be there,

paddling, spinning the raft. Who aren't there:
there's only Bernard Stams behind a house
that'll be torn down soon for a highway
the city's extending. We're college kids,

home for the holidays, out for a night, a bunch
of pals from high school. "Got any love,"
Stams asks. Sure, there are girls, but no
love. "There's this one chick," I say. Stams

knows the deal, knows I'm gone, a river rat,
set to become a dessert or appetizer among
the main dishes of America—a macaroon,
a special cheese. He was our center, he snapped

the ball, this thick, teddy bear of a Yale
double major—he understands things
from the middle. Now a mess of guys scoot
inside to see the mantis of Twenty-Three

on the tube—some breakaway—damns & shits
spilling from the sliding glass. Stams pulls up
his jeans, faded just right, leers at the stars
where the millions he'll make is written,

as it was for his father, as it will be for his son.
A chipmunk skitters in the ivy. "Who cooks
for you," asks a barred owl. Soon we'll find
ourselves in Jim's Tavern, the crowd congenially

skittish, college kids having one more
for how much we look forward to medical,
law, or business school—a house in town,
one in the country. Sure, some might break out,

escape from the escaping through another form
of escape, but for now a hard frost whispers
its way into the fescue, lights of the city
giving the stars a good run for their money.

II

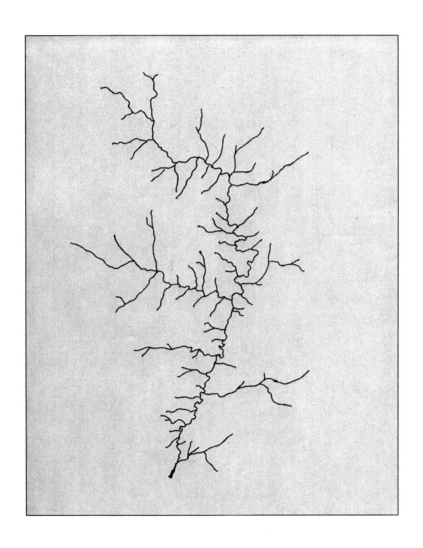

HIGH WATER

THE GUESSING LAND

1

Water in the ear, that's what we are.
We're not about rain. We're about the threat—

streak by spark, veins in some celestial leaf: listen,
the dogs of ether are howling, scratching the door.

2

Me the custodian of autumn rain, me
the mote in ash tree's flame. Hawks
crave my harassment, know my feathers
are green the way blue jay's are brown.
If I lie, ink me grander ones on branches
so new with nudity they seem breaks
in the clouds. What's true is what moves,
and those who worry it are stuck. Me
need them like the ancients needed goats
to keep the gods happy, themselves aloft.

3

I lift the day over the field's particular
depressions on a sheen as of the earth
having slept hard, or not slept, never slept,

and bend it long into shapes of land & of time
to be worn like a mood, that fleeting, light—
all ravishment, all nothingness, all ghost.

4

A kind of rapture
having maggots for eyes. I could see
to the other side of the sun,
where my tongue was living. But sight
is overrated. Often I was terrified
and ran into the woods, climbing all the trees
I couldn't name. Now everywhere
I am empty—my tail, pouch—
grows red. Now in my veins the clouds
congeal, albino leeches.

5

We're up again, tickling the world thirsty,
a whole culture, regal with etiquette,
style, ways of standing

and standing by. Earth-lick, dementia
of umbrella, drowned flesh. Slopeways,
a triangle of ten or so,

and when you walk in it, a strange energy
massages into your feet some extract.
Blithe basilicas in reds

and sulfur, what are we, monuments
to the end of drought, or the consciousness
of the understory?

Linger, we say, know your poison.

6

Flatulent with contour
squirm the embody wind   how ages
weather here   how I grovel
a pause a prescience time's speedtrap
churning the root   of stillness
a smash up   one substance
everywhere divisible

7

Black light, maggot rave —
I couldn't have been further from flight.
Already picked clean by flood
and by weather, & still
some relative circled. No creek
would cry me a river.

8

Am the eyes of heaven and the unspoken
unpinned; am blessed, shadow-licked,
pacing to the lay of the land, a thing
before joy, hurt, before mercy — seeds
from weeds that grow only in clouds.

9

Queen of waste place bouquets,
in March I stand,
stalks light as fungo bats—

scimitared heads, elaborate rattles.
Even my leaves hang on
wilted & mauve as though death

did not mean separation.
And, below, my offspring, nests
of fuzz & vein, no green

more pale save that of luna moth;
imagine, six feet later,
the candescent, cactus-like fire.

10

Trees' branchwork overshadows me,
but in firelight you've seen my double;
breathing, tasted it—least decorative,
protector & first to go: nothing
more servant to majesty.

11

You roll in me, & roll, but cannot wear my silence,
only the coming & going, the fascination
with a gleam so full of grace it disappears.

12

How, when crushed, we go mint,
go paste.

How ants comb our innermost,
that tassle,

that cob. You love us, the way
a flood loves

the bank by leaving silt as it recedes.
Let us spoon

you into the world's mouth after it prays,
devilishly.

13

Shabkar, that raven-braided yogin of Tibet,
said that to make an offering to a single hair
of one's master surpasses making offerings
to a thousand Buddhas. Hook me up, I say,
the big guys are bored by gifts, and we are more
than calligraphy on the lawns, streets, & bricks.

14

I am the between where you arrive most
aware, having forgotten enough to know.
I melt lines into shape, shape into music—
whippoorwill, bullfrog—the air cools,

breathes you. Time of the fullness of time,
when matter is deliverance, a way in, an out—
elements collide in me, colors vibrate
like answers to the riddle of the day.

𝕿 𝕾

1   *thunderstorm*
2   *crow*
3   *mist*
4   *opossum (roadkilled)*
5   *mushroom*
6   *wave*
7   *dead buzzard*
8   *rain*
9   *mullein*
10   *bark*
11   *dew*
12   *tulip poplar blossom*
13   *pine needle*
14   *dusk*

Fold Effect

Thus seeing   river means
mist not   mist Means
paths between   patches the
rise & drift   Wash yes
waveslap curdle   ism Very
pulse how un   stitched
Obsidian   taffied Sparkled
charcoal   very wrinkle

Happy Family

Four person raft: husband, wife, two kids—
the silence more tense than a green guide
at Corkscrew Rapid in high water. *Happy Family*,
we'll call them: you've seen it—eyes
like mercury, nobody saying what they think,
all decoding, the difference between
what's heard & what's said requiring a PhD.

in translation. I'd been pondering the accuracy
of the mother's nose & cheek when the father,
in reply to my asking, said that he worked as
a plastic surgeon. All day I took extra care
to show his kids the flowers, lead them
through underwater caves, erosion rooms,
turn rocks for salamanders, explain the gorilla

and raven faces in the lines on the cliffs. I can't
say they were excited, that their posture
was different at day's end on the bus back
to the outpost when the mother asked where
I'd grown up & hearing same neighborhood
and school as her kids, leered at her husband
who frowned or smiled, I couldn't tell.

EXFOLIATIVE

How sometimes in February
the trees would break
into spiral each time the wind sent a casserole
of hardened snow

through the limbs & vines—
you copied their script,
you touched the trunks, noted their hold,

certain inconsistencies of shape, the way the canopy exploded
as though with another pollen,
the old yearning for water.

Your father had a name for people like you.
It had been your oldest goal
to disappoint him.
Only now,

as the clouds squirmed,
you saw it plain as the bend in the branches—
he had a point. You were making it.

How fine to know
it was over, that part.

SOUTHERN CRESCENT

First light in Clemson: sweet gum, sudden suddenness:
        phlox in ditches, Slurpee of trumpet creeper—

a train, always looking, is always lost. Even
        at the crossroads of Yonah Mountain and County Line—

lost with its thin face, grimace and square eyes.
        See the runoff and fescue, red clay and pine.

Lost, and a long bone in the foothills near Toccoa;
        one arc of a parenthesis, the other the Atlantic—

Jekyll, Sapelo. All night we cut through the dark
        like insomnia; High Point, Salisbury—the windows

weren't the only eyes: here a cement truck, there
        an H&R Block, houses with lights on, most without.

Everything was static, even the motion—steel
        on steel. Time birthed itself in the lurch and grind.

Green glow at stoplights. A Citgo, a Waffle House.
        Two men discussed real estate, another snored.

What did the rail insist that thought reverted
        to rain—dust, falling; that it's not the tracks

that bear us, but the ties? Sentimental, yes,
        but mother I'm coming to see you. I hope

your paperwhites are blooming in the glass bowl
        on the dinner table, dangerous with fragrance

of lemon and honey, stalks a density easy
    to hide behind as I leaned over the spoonfuls

of grits you always served more than the stomach
    could take. You never pointed to the roots wormy

and white at the bulges of scalloped glass,
    never to the one bud close to breaking

as though from birth to final waking, but offered
    more meat, more spicy Velveeta grits. Mother,

is that woman who was my mother gone,
    is her song more thrush now than chickadee,

will I miss her inchoate leaps of mind,
    mistake her freedom as the truest gift? Dad's fine.

The others are fine. You're leaving him, fine.
    We had to accept it in order to live

at all, and we did in time, as if that was
    the gift. There's blue in the sky now,

some brighter chapter of gray. Tankers
    slow with oil lumber north. Always looking,

always lost; and vultures, a few hoods up
    at the Brake & Lube; Piedmont miraculous with haze,

summer's heavy equipment: candelabra of saw palmetto,
    sumac, kudzu. Lost, and ninety degrees in Buford,

and the smoking car full, and yarrow, and mullein;
    and Atlanta, fast and shiny and breathing hard.

Section Zero

But who will break camp here
after catering exuberance's wedding;
who will ride off on the horse

that remorse unsaddled?
Ignore the persimmon innard,
the tonic & turnstile,
the christmas fern—elope's a fine bride
if being cosmic floats
your tennis shoe. Besides,

how many colonies
can one ear sustain? How many times
can deficiency & surplus
lock tongues? It's a zoo,

or a rip in it, some etherzone,
things bedded down

in order to burst. Hard to say,
harder to fell
the would so it rots to will.
Say so. It's early,
but blossom-musk has turned before
on its bellydance,
pierced the nose. See the graffiti
of sapsucker, the abdomen
that calls greenbriar its silk—what about

the sycamore, positioned
like a missionary
among the heathenous glow.

WHERE WE LIVED, WHERE WE GOT PAID

Mostly it was some guy's tax write-off,
though he might have seen it much nobler
like he was saving the world or something.

Maybe he was. Maybe mine. Worlds
are funny, only one & always one more.
Mostly he was a guy named Rick or Clarke,

one syllable I'm sure. A lawyer, mostly.
How does it go? Once a lawyer always
a lawyer, the way Mazzie on my first

training trip said of guiding, *first you
do it for fun, then you do it for friends,
then you do it for money.* A warning,

I see now. Who knows? Maybe he saw it
as a refuge for people in the steel trap
of adolescence, unable to take the leap.

Sure, we were stuck, nursing our wounds,
heros all day, river gods, or some shit.
Mostly he knew it was safe, kegs

most nights, sporty, ridiculous fucking
we'd call Tantric. Sometimes I say this
to make it go away, or stay. I don't know.

Mostly it comes out a different shade
of the same; this was the South after all,
the bruised South, a commune that had once

been a country music park: always there
was singing, somebody in tears—always
a whippoorwill, somebody with a gun.

Hacky Sack as Euphoric Recall

One no-see-um-thick evening, when the sun
is a basketball going down
through a dense stand of hardwoods,
we will stand, you & I,

with minds rendered lard
by bong hits, and witness a woman
—a perfect stranger—yabadabadoo
a woven sack of beads

above the ground with her feet. There will be nothing
apologetic about the way we stare
as she juggles the footbag, no shame
in our gawking at the way she snaps it—

right knee, left knee—through a dusk
made disco-mythic
by the jackpot hazard lights
of our gazes; no, what we share

will be pure
reproachless, unselfconscious, downright
ecstatic pleasure
in the way she spinespanks it

into the crux between breast & breast,
holds the stall, and, then,
as if there had never been a question
about loving life, plunks it

to the outside of her foot, corkscrewing
her whole, splendiferous thigh inward, hands
to the side, head down, bad hair
sluicing through the sun's three-pointer light.

If Not Weather

Always wombfulness to go by,
if by means aciding
the anchor's chain. This lexicon, this

porridge—it's simple:
delicious says *quiet down*. But so
the tempter returns,
the world
turns fungus, the soil

its hop,

and then—bacterial sky,
oak's parchment

like slits in the whatnot. Zany
how each breath palpates, becomes a soul
or doesn't, how sounds
repeal themselves

in a muffle like traffic, the sky flaring
its nostrils only
to jimmy up
the mudlurid. Take the garlic mustard—
Alliaria officinalis,
its liverous collard-veins—
press it to your neck. Hold it

there. See,

the rain hasn't arrived, but sends word
of its departure
idwardly.

BEGINNING TO PEEL

To lay among the pale stations
of maple leaves in a breeze,
the ground a soft bedding
where wild ginger mingles
with cleavers and mayapple
in patches so dense it seems
the cyclopic blossoms need
no light but that which oozes
from leaf-rot & old nut husks,
their hulls upturned as though
dragged from moorings by
the spring tide; to lay, watching
the shadows flicker & sway,
letting the oaks' hair fall, strand
by pollenacious strand, fall,
little ticklers, on the tough meat
of our necks; warmer air spilling
from the sun-anointed fields,
is to feel our stems burn
to a vain, lusty pink, selfless
with desire somehow, bark
beginning to peel, long,
sclerotic mats. Spores collect
in our nooks & cavities, sap
like a bleeding outward
beneath archipelagos
of mold, coal-black & crusty.
What are our bodies now
if not a spangling of veins
deaf to all vision save
the worship of flesh by tongue,

eyes, even closed, puddles
where frogs are swimming
and singing & staying alive?

Spittoono Lily

Copenhagen, Kodiak, Grizzly, Skoal—
Lily dipped them all, loved the brown shreds of leaf
as they swashed against her tongue, escapees
from the den of lip & gum,

and it was nearly as meaningful
when she was young, stealing pinches in the corner,
training the gut to handle reflux & burn
so she could get away

with it in Algebra One, where Mrs. Rowland
never taught nicotine or the brain's strange charity,
how multiplied they equal calm, focus,
and ill, being a rebel

at that straitjacket of a school. Later,
so she could find the freshest tin, Lily moved
to Nashville where the finest, Copenhagen,
is made. That moist softness

between index and thumb, feeling her face
purse like old fruit in hot sun, nearly rivals sex, Lily said
on our last date, and, anyway, she clipped, since
everyone knows life's

hazardous to health, isn't addiction
synonymous with love. Lily's drained gallons
of saliva since that contest in Clemson—
Spittoono, they called it

(she won)—but if she gets to its cousin
in Charleston, I hope she doesn't spit anymore
gently or discreetly, but enjoys the motions
of dancers as that other dance

tunes the dark orchestras of her blood.

Trees & Stars

Silly raft, craft without the c —
add water & testosterone,
and you have the day I led

four strange folks from Orlando
down the Chattooga River. *What
do you mean the river doesn't*

do a circle, the first guy asked,
when I told him not to leave
his wedding band under a rock

at the put-in. He was serious
and so was his buddy who said
who put the rocks here, why

*don't we see more wildlife,
this isn't what the brochure
made it out to be.* As if the burger

we're served is as perfect
as the one pictured in the menu.
Why do the trees get taller farther

from the river? was a question
so obvious & Zen-pretzelled
it stumped me. One guy, all day,

paddled backward when I said
forward, & vice versa, probably
didn't like my cool, neo-hippie

attitude. It was weird but this
was March, a weird month,
and when I showed them a trillium

up the drainage at Long Creek,
guess what?—they asked who
planted it. Probably a bird, I said,

or the wind. Not long after this
on a long trip I was leading
a kid freaked out. It was late

and we were under the stars, &
they were shooting. In his calf,
he'd been shot, in a drive-by

before a string of lock-ups,
the latest, for possessing a quarter
ounce of weed, which was why

he was with me for thirty days
of backpacking—not boot camp,
just hauling a big bag & trying

to be good. About the stars, what
could I say? It was cold
and we needed sleep, so I told

the story about the folks
from Orlando on the river,
and how ridges like the one

we were camped on top of
make the trees look taller
than they really are.

HIGH WATER

Begin by Licklog Creek's last cascade,
at its confluence with the Chattooga,
where ions trundle their positive charges

against stacks of slippery, mica-lit schist.
Here the river exposes its film
below those bosom buddies,

the hemlock & Virginia pine;
and the sedge, azalea, & Joe Pye weed
sway in their meditation,

having almost hitched a ride
last night with Hurricane Danny.
You have to love the plants

that hang on midstream,
the ferns, laurel, & doghobble,
the patience of moss, humility of lichen;

You have to love the grottoes, wolf-spidered
and intimate, all the colors, odors, patterns,
universal & ambivalent; the slow orbit

of rhododendron blossoms past
the driftwood heap; the eddy's dark
clockwork; the erratic pulse

of the curling waves, the way
the rocks tell the water
where & how to go,

even as the water eats them edgeless,
pothole by pothole,
grain by swirling grain.

Chattooga River Trail, April

Just four miles to camp, the trail flat, so at lunch break
on some nameless monolith of gneiss between Fall Creek
and Thrift's Ferry, two kids, Eduardo & Terrell, I think—

they all run together now—& Liza Beth, my co-instructor
swam below the shoals, an easy moving pool, enough current
to force us downstream as we crossed, but not far, or far

enough that we felt tough & clean. Day twenty-one: forget
that Eduardo on day six had jacked off in my hat, then
after an apology & three nights solo, brawled tooth & nail

with Scott over a cigarette butt they'd found on the trail.
Forget my power trips, the hubris of thinking I had a thing
to teach save how to adjust a backpack, set up a tight, dry

sleeping tarp, where was a safe place to swim. The water
felt like being inside a daffodil just as the petals open, all
butter & frill. Sure, it was chilly, April, but this was Georgia,

no, South Carolina now that we were on the other side, watching
a catfish, a seven incher, writhe gill-deep in a water snake's jaw,
the one sliding onto the beach I thought we'd have to ourselves.

If You Liked Your Ride, Tip Your Guide

Gratuities are accepted
but not expected
—sign in a store

When the guests came out of the showers,
hung their wetsuits, slipped on dry shoes,
they found us lined up on the benches

like dogs in the kitchen after a meal.
Yes, wag. Always that creek squirming
behind us sounded more hurried then,

but was never more slow. We might
as well have held cups out. That's how
lewd it felt. Maybe we deserved it.

Don't waitpeople, barbers? Fives, tens,
often wet, we'd get. Sometimes. One
never knew. It was awkward for them,

and many palmed the cash in a handshake
along with an address or business card
as if it wasn't old fashioned to think

that people who'd spent a good day
on the river might keep in touch.

III

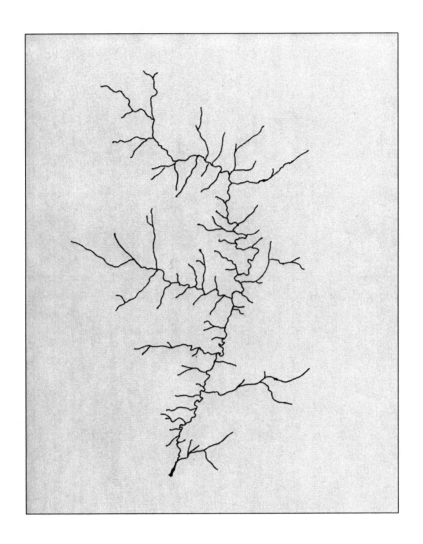

MAKING A MAP

MAKING A MAP OF THE RIVER

It wasn't tracing so much as drawing by sight,
and went best when I didn't watch
my hand, only the lines on the original page,
feeling the river splash between eye,
memory, wrist, & pen. Picturing each bend

from my boat again, or from the trail
drew me off, two inches where a half
should have been, or less.

I left it blank, just the river's line,
some major tributaries, no names, roads,
or topographical relief.

Not even a north.

RISKING BREAD

Honeysuckle stuck in its mania of twining,
spiders plump as they'll get, their webs
ragged with inedibles — leaf bits, old legs:
here is the broken ground,

the hinge on which seasons squeak
like crickets or towhees, like life run down,
some new rapture at hand, worldrubble
blistered with what's possible

and what's not. Slowly, ripeness swallows
its tongue, turning gray to blues where
violent, healing clouds recline; slowly
and with ease, like the trees

giving blood again, who say the way to water
is a flower in the weeds, who say it's time
to scrap the gaudy halos and live like home
is the dough we knead,

even if the bread is loathe
to rise, even if the heart must be plucked
to grow new feathers, a gut-smart beak,
hardened wings.

Dead Man's Pool

Another slow afternoon on the drift—
a little moth traffic, egg
of a hickory nut in the leaves.
I catch it while I can,
the birdsong's vagrant topographies,
turtle surfacing
like a visitor from another earth. I catch it
in my chest, the hollows there, the vines
with their gummy fruits, and then—quick lateral—
I pitch it. Maybe you
have some running room, know
from having escaped it
the anatomy of pity,
and can swim through the sweet lanes
of the poplar's roots,
your hair stronger than hope,
as drenched.

*

Pliny, when he died at Pompeii,
43 AD, pillow on his head to soften the blows
from Vesuvius's tirade—
the pumice, superballs
of lava, flame—it was another morning. His heart,
not eight miles in diameter
(but big enough), also blew its lid. Now here:
nowhere—it matters
little alone
or all one, because the jewelweed burns,
niblet of saffron

a tender magma, and the river poked
with scum amoebaing almost
salivates the unknowing
with a silence you can hear beneath
dawn's gauze, that pimpling,
that pulse.

*

Listening says smell
the mushroom for a change. So
I do. It
stinks, burns the nose. All
the trees in
those caves go up
in orange glow. It's hot. The river
flames browner,
a cinnamoning
course, a
strafe sleeveless & queer. But, say,
where
for all that quivering do
the leaves attain
the mercy
—encrimsoning—to
remain?

In the Narrows

I like the vine-thick crevices in the Narrows
of the Chattooga, first leaves — it's March —
maybe they are fox grape, and wolf spiders;
the lowbush blueberry's red bells, hummocks
of bluets & moss, fallen holly leaves gold
as monarchs banking, a little off balance
or on, and flies.
        Who says a river has no tide
need watch swallows flit in cliffs like
attention itself, sandpipers in sandpockets,
fiddleheads of the broad beech. Need stand
among the hackberry, it's wormy nodes,
and chew on the maple's samara the way
memory does gnaw your bitters clean.

Dream of My Father

To get upstream, not to the source
  but somewhere close enough
to smell its gifts and risk
  being forgiven, my father
made a pole, whittled a length
  of cedar. The shavings,
they reeked of urine at first;
  with air, with time, they softened,
and he cupped them to his face
  as though they'd speak, as though
he'd hear them with his nose.
  Water, he heard, broken water
was all he could taste. One
  might say it was long, that
the work consumed him,
  but he took it slow enough
to be quick and he failed
  perfectly. The scrap was soil
soon and my father too,
  but near the end, when
he hauled the tired body
  of his canoe on the shore
for the last time and handed
  the pole to me, the wood
was smooth with use, and in
  a voice meant for roots,
worms, cooler, darker heavens,
  he said, "The tree when growing
had hardly been straight
  and once carved was even
more bent, but it brimmed

with moon and grape and translated
the bottom of the river
    for my ignorant hands." I shook
his right one then, still know
    like the itch after a sting
that pulse of stone, grain—
    a gentle, sinuous gift & custody.

OCTOBER SLOW DRIFT

Alder, spicebush, hemlock:
dwarf white pine, dwarf maple—
not an island,
          but a resistance
of gneiss,
pyrite-bright, squigular & kingfishered;
you know the habit
          such rockingbirds wear.
You see the work of scour
in stone, of grind & grain—

the algae that sets up, the dampdark,
things warty, catkinesque.

＊

Vessel & shore,
          cursive & thorn—as if
pebbles in a coffee can,
licked lips:
          let it strip you, traveler,

the brass of light sandlensed,
those lungerays, lines
          the mouth makes
& rides, that gutteral vista;

          let it strip, let it dissolve you
to utter root.

＊

River oats poke & tremor,
their posture an inquisitive nod—
ironwood above them, maple above that—

reds the color of sulking,
indecision's orange, and calm,
the yellow of calm, yellow of sun

in brush, decay's yellow, of the meridian
between green & brown,
beast & angel, a river & its range.

*

Sandbar, boulder,
sunburst on water's fold.

Traffic of flies, some hatch, caddis perhaps.
Now silk, a good strand, drifts

over the beach, the canoe, paddle
stuck in sand. Almost mirror,

the ripples on the bottom. Meanwhile,
midriver's olivemerald, slow here

yet adamant in its course.
Meanwhile, pressure points on pressure. Vortices.

Squirrel swims across, squirrel!
None of it without ease.

*

Late-blooming lobelia,
black-capped chickadee on broken
yellow pine. Dragonfly, cutbank—

snatches of bottom, snatches of depth
and murk—a suspension, horizonless,
as though looking into sky:
scalloped sand, halibuts
of sunkleaves.

*

Afternoon & I've set up camp
on a spit two islands above Sandy Ford.

Sit, paddle, walk.
Sleep, swim, paddle.

A good day, lonesome & sweet.
Sun teed up on the pine-canopied ridgeline,

milky way of gnats in the shine,
the sand soft & the mud softer—

wisdom of driftwood in branch & trunk.
In this light, the river is bluebrown.

And grey, gunmetal, like the trout spotted earlier
when the world was evergreen.

Say there's a beaver, an old t-shirt in the sand. Say world.
Say anything. Unspeak every word.

Off Broadway

When the four wheel drive bus that once
hauled workers to the Alaska Pipeline
dropped its transmission on the road
out of the gorge, Holwood climbed

from the roof, from his lounge chair
in the ratcheted stack of rafts,
and ushered the guests aside where
they contained their patience

like so many microwaved tin cans.
He'd been thinking of the low power line
on Damascus Church Rd., and how
riding the roof, he'd better duck there

or lose his head, but now he was
out of it, doing a hillbilly version
of "To be or not to be," his voice
as granitic as the pool below Corkscrew,

each word compressed up the slinky
of his throat—"whether tis nobler
in mind to suffer," Boss Hog as Hamlet,
but a ponytail now, lifejacket,

Jesus sandals. Meanwhile I fixed
a game of balance with rope & bail buckets,
but nobody noticed it, with Holwood's stylus
jumping to "Sarah Cynthia Stout,"

then "Billie Potts;" the guests, some
of them helmeted still, bobbing
with his gestures, the sluice of syllables,
as if they were the story, & they were the story.

WITH SOPHIE, AGE TWENTY MONTHS,
AT WOODALL SHOALS

I think the river had sand in its eyes
that day, wee vertebrae of sky
in each riffle.

Of course the sun
had its high beams on. Of course
we played hopscotch in the mica-studded sand.

Later, your mother's face, when she emerged
from a dip,
was marigold, no, a garnet

in the conglomerate of us.
Later, dressed in armor of holly leaves,
we chased sweat bees

through the smooth, blue basilicas of granite,
and you only cried a little bit
going down for a nap.

Near Sandy Ford

Might as well go swimming as try to sing another river song,

might as well roll up my jeans
as say the mist resembles cloud wax
or steam from the land's boiling kettle.

I'll do that later. Listen

to these ledges—
not that they're even or uniform or even
ledges so much as humps & bumps, miniatures of tolerance
after a night on the town—listen to their milky harmonics,
as if a guitar strung with snakes;

and to the muscadines on the trail,
their thick skin & stench, and the way that pine hangs

over the point
on the inside of the bend, hemlock beyond it & mist
and the outside of another bend, so many S's—

the needles it puts in your neck,
the dead limbs, the frill.
Listen. There's time

for a few good words and even some bad ones
before another swim.

DIXIE CUP

Flashback: Chattooga River, March, dogwoods
sharpening their milky flags
in the woolen, cloud-weary sun,

and Holwood—bearded, unwashed—
in Jawbone, in the Watauga Chute, kneels
in a We-No-Nah Edge, a boomerang

of a canoe, rockered
for slalom gates, a Frankie Hubbard
hand-me-down, an itchy, splintery ride, as much

Duct-Tape as Kevlar; Holwood Sloan,
my mentor, the one
who showed me another way

to breathe, feathering his blade,
umbilically—draw, cross-forward, brace—
in the Chattooga's green tea,

past Decapitation Rock, holding
the angle, thinking
like a Dixie Cup, like

he'd tell me to think
in Idaho that July above
six miles of logjam

and runoff called
Unforgiveness Gorge, a name so dramatic
it's silly, & real. You've pissed in them,

right? Sipped spring water
while waiting for some appointment—
bank, dentist, barber:

Dixie Cups. God,
those sodden years of marijuana,
mushrooms, adrenaline, beer

became a way of life I'm always
swimming from. Last night when my wife
explained that mothering

is wearing her out, that she needs
me to work more, work less,
I'm telling you it felt

like an attack
but wasn't and I wished
like a child I was

in my boat
but wasn't. Maybe we're all, each day,
hurled into a corner

that only crushing
the Dixie Cup, or filling it
with tears

will get us out of—
but which? Holwood, I heard,
married again, left

that bus he was living in
on a clearcut in Sumter National Forest
and is restoring barns

upstate. I've been
meaning to call him for some while.

BENDS

Downstream, the water turns to milk. A frog wriggles
in a snake's mouth. The rocks are still warm downstream
and a wolf spider hunkers like the story of a river

that begins downstream. It's March here, but it's April
there and the mayflies are going nowhere, it seems.
If you must say something important, say it quietly

and with your eyes and say it in the pines downstream.
Maybe belief's command is lean downstream, maybe
love is all end and beginning in the bends downstream.

Local Weather

Early February, Whetstone Bend, big red maple
on river right, its twig-ends laced with flowerish buds
frilly & scarlet like lost lures. Forget the gravel bar,

the sludge-dark stones, silt & leaves nearly silt.
Forget the mussel shells, the canoe pulled up there,
mud & sticks below the seat. Today is beyond itself,

or behind, in two weathers at once, as if the same
music played concurrently, at different speeds. I've poled
past beaver dams, branches fresh-gnawed, their

cambium gleam brighter than the sky, a local glow.
In the mud-soft bluffs are many days like this: wheeze
of dove wings, always a corpse—coon, doe. As though

the eyes at the bottom of the river could see right
through heaven. As if the current could go either way.
I like these days, how confusion flirts with symmetry,

the vultures' double high fives, ferns on the north slope,
each clump another time zone. See the outcrop, stumprot—
things soft despite the drought. Here doghobble mocks

the moon's wax. Here vines overspiral, aspiring
to purest circle. For hours, or what seem like hours,
thought drifts, a little off balance, up the tributaries

of the day's changing breeze—now from the southwest,
now from the east—a day that's turned its other cheek
and winked the wink of something going under—muskrat,

hellgrammite. Nothing breeds in the runout, in the eddies
& pools, but reflection-static, those worn out rhymes &
reasons. No bugs emerge, no carpenter bees or beetles

from the whittled wood of breathing. It feels good out here,
like grieving, scratching some pity ticket, hanging
that wet wool, hanging it out. I like it. As if somebody

way up there was trolling & I was the bait, as if somebody
was framing a window & I wasn't the sawdust, wasn't
the sunk nail, but the skin that clams up the hammer grip.

A Little River, a Little Flame

It sounds like somebody's tearing through
a bag of crumpled paper.
And then there are treefrogs & crickets
in waves of whirr & purr.
Also, rain drips on the tarp, spelling sleep,
though it's barely legible.
Earlier we swam, brief swims in briefs
or less. We waded, hopped.
You conjure now little flames like blossoms
from the shallow pit
with hemlock snips & breath. You kneel,
rings glowing, synthetic
turtleneck zipped up, and speak of pain
in the body, how it hurts
to hurt so much every day. Our child sleeps
in a tent near the river
where the water could be somebody tearing
through a bag of paper,
crumpling it. Lately, specialists
have tossed the names
of maladies like so much paper in a bag
somebody's tearing through
and through. Everything is blazes. You toss
another stick on the coals
where orange does the wave. The river laughs.
Even ash is a kind of flower.

Overflow

Holwood and Larson offered to show us down Overflow Creek, a steep tributary of the Chattooga that in normal weather, even moderately wet, was too low for boating. It had been raining for days, steady and hard. Big low pressure off the Gulf, remnants of hurricane. The river was closed to commercial rafting. Too high, few eddies.

So all that water dropped quick and furious, and so green under a low roof of foliage, I was about to go crazy just from looking around. Maybe I already had that summer. I don't know anymore. We got baked on the way up the old logging road, and we got baked again once we got there, had unloaded our boats and were considering turning back. Holwood and Larson grew good dope in clearcuts throughout the National Forest. They'd introduced Mazzie, Alice, and me to running waterfalls on the Tellico, Chauga, Section Zero, Watauga, and the Upper Nantahala. Like Larson and Holwood, Mazzie and I enjoyed being high when we paddled steep stuff. It both soothed and gave our nerves a new edge. Alice never needed it. Years have passed since I saw her, but I bet she still doesn't smoke and paddle, as she always seemed close enough to the water.

We were scared. It was part of creeking. What you did with that fear. A blown move, being one inch off your line, could be deadly; at the least, highly inconvenient. Walking out of the gorge took a full day in itself.

In the eddy below a drop—there had been six-footer leading into a twelve—Alice looked at me. We'd both lost our angle on the approach, I had flipped and rolled. The creek was running full, near the max level for boating. I saw her eyes were green where they had once been brown. She smiled. I was a wreck of adrenaline, and said something corny like "Wow."

Alice screeched wildly, blissfully; made a noise like a cougar, then peeled out first to run the next one, a thirty-footer named Singley's Falls.

For the next two hours, running the seven miles through the near continuous drops, Alice, Mazzie, Holwood, Larson, and I didn't say a word; we only made animal noises—tweets and roars, hisses and coos. Wolf, bird, snake, locust, everything great and small. Growling, whistling, we did all kinds of wacky with our throats to the air coming out of them.

But none of this is important. What matters is we lived.

INSIDE THE RIVER

Though he is older now,
though he is tired and lives
far from that place and woman,
he sometimes wakes up
in the dark and reads
by the light their bodies made
that night inside the river,

the pothole where in spring
at higher flows a man swept
from his canoe had flushed,
been trapped, as they were,
in their skin, water running over—
luminous roof—some pumping in:

so many tongues. She said
there was a whippoorwill
in her pelvis. He said his cock
was foxfire. No, she said,
a rainbow trout. Somewhere
in that watershed, the chestnut trees

stood up again and grew
several unnecessary inches.
Maybe a stonefly hatched.
Blood is ninety percent water,
she said. Then I want you
dry, he replied, I want you

in a warm, sturdy bed. Later,
she promised, and then

in some thick place of doghobble,
mica, yellowroot, where
the mind scores its banks,
where the dusky salamanders
of desire feed, and the rocks

could care less for a future
of sand, a dead man found
his canoe and was mouthing
the same words her left nipple spoke
when it puckered against his lips —
whose hunger, whose song?

IV

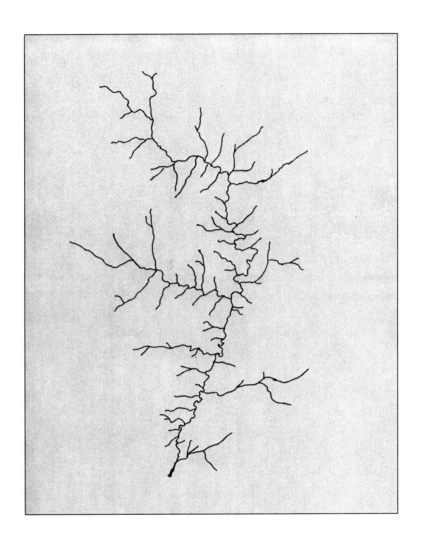

CHATTOOGA MIND

Chattooga Mind

I AM KNEELING in a canoe that spins in a pool below a bend in the Chattooga River. It is night. The pool is a garden of upwellings. Moonglow oozes from every stone and grain of stone and dimple and wave. The room-sized boulders just upstream compress the river into two narrow slots. There are waves. The water runs, the waves stay in place. You can hear them. They sound like an engine, like a lot of engines, but mostly they sound like time.

The river corridor against the horizon is toothy with the profile of hemlocks and pines. I stroke infrequently, aiming for quiet. I cannot see the bottom, just as I cannot assemble the river's individual noises. There are dripsounds, pulses and murmurs of liquid. There is a sound as of oil in a hot skillet. There are many other sounds. Night is in no hurry and neither is the cold. Details surrender to other, more amorphous details.

There is a cliff face on one side of the pool. Sixty feet across, a sandbar makes the other border. My sleeping bag, a dark shape, sprawls there, gathering dew that by morning will be frost in the places where my body wasn't touching it.

This bend in the Chattooga River has a name: Three Roostertails. The name includes its boulders of gneiss and schist and granite. It includes the doghobble and laurel hells on the banks, the saplings, the fallen trees, the long depressions where they're rotting—the thick moss and humus. It includes the histories of the Cherokee, of settlers, battles, of loggers, politicians, artists, mothers, children—all of us. It includes much more: wolf spiders, hellgrammites, salamanders, driftwood, raccoons, sandpipers, water, stars. So much more.

A man I'll call Norris Campbell built a shack in the woods somewhere above Three Roostertails. It is on the South Carolina-side of the river—that much I know. I worked with Norris during the years I guided rafts on this river. He wasn't your typical

National Forest land squatter. He was outgoing, clean-cut, mostly law-abiding, and good-humored. He is as much a part of Three Roostertails as the all the rest for which it is named.

Rising at two forks, one of them near Cashiers, North Carolina, the other near Scaly Mountain, Georgia, the Chattooga grows to form the border between Georgia and South Carolina, becoming, with confluences and a series of dams, the Savannah River. In terms of gradient, the Chattooga is the mildest of the seven lush waterways draining the tail end of the Appalachian chain, part of a landform called the Southern Blue Ridge Escarpment. But it isn't exactly mild. There are many places upstream and downstream of Three Roostertails where the water and the rocks combine in such a way as to have earned a name.

This is the first night of two in a thirteen-mile solo canoe trip down section three of the Chattooga. From the moment I started schlepping canoe and gear down the access trail at Earl's Ford several hours ago, I was enveloped by the landscape, its parts and the sum of its parts. I felt the pressure and presence of the place. It wrung me like a damp rag.

I come to the Chattooga to remember where I come from. I also come to check on the place. I like to see what has changed and what has stayed the same. The lineage that goes beyond recent generations is palpable here; it feels as urgent as my own history with the place and with the people of the place and their histories with the river. In 1990, just before my nineteenth birthday, I came to the Chattooga to learn how to guide rafts. For the next ten years, I led trips by foot, canoe, and raft through the watershed. I am only beginning to know the place.

AFTER FITFUL SLEEP, I wake to a cold morning. It is March, the eve of spring equinox. The sun oozes like uncertainty through the clouds. To get the blood moving, I scramble over boulders and flood-orphaned logs and walk the bottomland above the bend in the river upstream. There are flowmarks in the duff, remnants of a post-hurricane, high water day last fall when my buddies paddled through here. Most who guide rafts grow to love the sport of whitewater paddling. Whether we acknowledge it or not, being in a small craft allows a more intimate engagement with the water than sitting in a raft can do. It nourishes something perhaps as modern in us as primitive.

So last fall these folks paddled the thirteen miles from Earl's Ford to the bridge at Highway Seventy-Six when the river was running at 20,000 cubic feet per second. To compare this morning's flow of roughly eight hundred c.f.s with that day's maelstrom is like comparing the energy from a firecracker with that of a dirty bomb. I've heard several accounts of the river that day, of boats and paddles breaking, of long swims, of logs turning end over end, long down times, adrenaline-induced euphoria, and of hydraulics large enough to stop school buses. People who paddle such water are not foolish, but they are as close to it and as beautiful as any pilgrims. The stories they share, the river stories, are nearly as important as being on the water.

Twenty feet above the waterline there are saplings. They are bent and stripped. Most of them are budding, despite how combed with leaves and twigs from the autumn's high water. They give me another account of that flood, a little quieter but no less dramatic. I veer in my walk from the riverbottom and wander up a mixed hardwood cove. The vegetal, mineral stench of galax and laurel and soil runs through me in waves. My nose rides the aromas as my feet and eyes dowse the lines of tree and branch, ridge and drainage. I wonder about Norris. Last I heard he was living in Colorado. But someone else heard he was back in Greenville, caring for his mother. I keep an eye out for his dwelling. It is nowhere to be seen. I decide that I prefer it that way.

I HEAD DOWNSTREAM after breaking camp. It feels good to be back in the canoe. I try to paddle with as little effort as possible. I try to let the river do the work. The water is a good level for canoe camping—not too high, not too low. There's a plastic box of gear—clothes, sleeping bag, food—fastened by a rope between the middle thwarts. I'm usually a sloppy packer, tossing things where they'll land, but I'll encounter a few rapids that make the precaution of a box and rope necessary. I don't want to sleep in a wet bag or lose anything to the bottom of the river.

It is strange to think that I am breaking the law. Forest Service regulations require two boats per party on the Chattooga and that you fill out a permit to let them know when you left and from where, and where you will take out. I am okay with paying the fine if I am caught paddling alone with no permit. It is worth it to me. There is a sense, likely false, that I'm too alone to be alone. I like being alone in the woods because it makes me more careful. Being careful helps me begin to see and feel the world with the attention it deserves.

A water thrush spills its tinny, mellifluous call. Crows banter, a few of them high above the corridor. I see a hiker on the Georgia side of the river, at a place where the river is wide, Dicks Creek entering there with all the unassuming drama of a sixty foot sliding waterfall, pine log parked in the middle of it, sending water in yet another direction of fan and froth. What they call Dicks Creek Ledge extends bank to bank, and at today's water level consists of six slots. I choose the middle one and snake through the passages between boulders, surfing the waves, using the eddylines as best I can to turn the heavy boat.

My right shoulder reminds me of its past injury—it isn't pushy about it, but it gives me little take it easies. I dislocated it a few years back in one of those boats that demands a skirt and looks very much like Tupperware. Injuries to the shoulder are common to paddlers of such boats. So it goes. I keep on. The river keeps on. I look for the driest lines through the rapids. The sun is a disc through the clouds. End of winter smells, a cool breeze from the east. I think about the new logs that I saw washed in the jam at the head of the island above Sandy Ford earlier. I caught an eddy there and climbed on them. I think about their shapes, how they seemed the embodiment of every living thing the drainage and corridor has known. A river is not the same river twice; it is more than twice because the ways of its evaporation and subsequent falling and return to air and cloud change again and again.

I WORRY ABOUT the Chattooga. People assume it is protected because it was one of the first rivers to be designated under the National Wild and Scenic Rivers Act of 1968. One feels the illusion of a healthy watershed due to the quarter mile corridor on both banks that's protected from development of any sort. People assume the river will remain wild. The problem is the Chattooga is not as healthy or as wild as it deserves to be. That our standards for wild places have been compromised is just as problematic. Many think a river is fine when trucks, four wheelers, and golf carts aren't galloping down its banks, when tract mansions or single-wides or clearcuts aren't marring the view and—more importantly—the non human life of the ridges, hillsides, skies, and banks. Thankfully, I am not alone in having a different view of the matter.

There is no doubt the Chattooga is a pretty river and wilder than most that share such close proximity to Atlanta. There are real threats, however, and many of them are already harming the watershed. Runoff from Clayton, Georgia's sprawl into the major tributary Stekoa Creek dumps silt and pollution into the river with or without heavy rain. The Forest Service allows large timber cuts that border the Wild and Scenic corridor. A quarter mile is not enough distance to cushion the erosive effects of clear cutting and road building. That the costs of these cuts do not equal the costs of the timber's sale, meaning the taxpayers bear the burden, does not trouble me as much as the fact that these cuts ruin habitat. These examples only scratch the surface.

Many have watched the damage to the watershed's health magnify over the years. There are individuals and organizations

such as the Chattooga Conservancy and Forest Watch who work
to minimize these threats. Sometimes they are successful. Their
battles are frequent and ongoing, their opponents muscled with
greed. I am awed by the faith and vigilance of folks like Butch
Clay, Buzz Williams, Nicole Hayler, and the many others who
battle on the front lines of environmental justice. Buzz, the
director of the Chattooga Conservancy, told me that conservation
work is pushing him towards becoming a real estate agent. We do
what we have to do. Buzz needs private individuals and groups to
purchase and preserve what land comes for sale in the watershed.
You should see this robust, sagacious man, a former Forest Service
employee, when he says with an alarming lack of pity that it is the
only way to save the river anymore.

The Chattooga deserves more protection than what's prescribed
by its Wild and Scenic status. I don't believe it is too much too ask
the legislators and agencies to protect the integrity of the entire
upper watershed. There are simply not enough waterways in the
Southeast that are so intact, where one can get a sense of the earth
primeval. We need to amend the Chattooga's Wild and Scenic
status to include all of its tributaries and to expand the corridor
that encompasses them. We need to designate as Wilderness Areas
the vast roadless tracts near Three Forks and Rock Gorge. We
need to enact a moratorium on road-building and logging within
the watershed, just as landowners and businesses there deserve
incentives to minimize impact.

Forest management policies, driven by corporate pressures, are
stripping efforts at conservation. In May of 2005, our government
repealed the roadless initiative, which opened hundreds of acres
of roadless area in the Chattooga watershed to road building and
logging. On a larger scale, the 60 million acres of roadless land
across the U.S. that were relatively safe from heavy logging before
this move, were now fair game. Once the lid was off the cookie
jar, the Forest Service was quick in implementing plans to harvest
more timber from national forests. Governors in Virginia, North

Carolina, and South Carolina, however, responded to public outrage at these moves by petitioning the feds to issue rules that would restrict road construction and timber harvesting on designated roadless areas. This was a start. The Chattooga is a tricky case because the first 56 miles below its source, the river's fragile infancy, is in the domain of three states and, therefore, three different Forest Service agencies, making it difficult to enact a much needed (and already drafted) comprehensive conservation plan for the watershed.

A LITTLE WATER splashes over the canoe's gunwale as I enter a rapid called the Narrows. I am shocked to see the fallen hemlock that dangled for years into a pothole on the river right bank is gone. High water, like time, leaves its mark by what it takes. I'm reminded of the fact that we really know our landmarks once they're washed away. After the first wave train, I carve into an eddy, pull the canoe ashore, and walk the boulders. An old boot in the sand, steel toed. Frog spawn, jellied blobs, in the pools on the boulder. A swallow flits among the cliffs.

As I explore the Narrows on foot, I remember swimming with my wife and daughter here two springs ago. I was living apart from Kirsten and Sophie then. It was a hard but necessary time. It wasn't easy, but marriage, indeed any effort at meaningful partnership is the antithesis of easy. When old raft guide friends, Christy and Chris Todd, who settled on Damascus Church Road, not far from the Section Four take-out, hiked in to visit our campsite at the bend above the rapid, I was floored by the generosity of their simple gesture. Our old pal, Lance Ellis, accompanied them. It was a warm April Saturday. The kids played in the mica-studded sand. We talked about whatever we talk about and what we talk about is the river. Mostly we listened. To each other. To the water. We shared the place.

Running the rest of the Narrows is, as usual, better than a dream. The canoe rocks and lurches and I with it. Water falls from the same rocks it always has, the seeps glimmering in the breaking and entering sun. The river churns as it emerges from under and between boulders, merging in so many bulging parentheses and pulsing whitecaps. When that hiker upstream at Dicks Creek asked me how far I was going, I fibbed. Savannah, I said. He smiled as though in tune with such wishful thinking.

Downstream apiece I portage Second Ledge, not wanting to risk a dump. I don't pack lightly. My battering ram of a big tandem boat, loaded with a heavy box of gear, is unpredictable when the river falls vertically, as it does for six feet or so at Second Ledge. But portages allow me to see the river in another way. I see the banks more closely, their curious blend of erosion and growth. Carrying my box of gear, I study the ground for solid footing and see the soil and stone, yellowroot and laurel and moss, things that tend to get overlooked when you're deep in the relationship of canoe and river.

I also look for signs of people—footprints, stray bits of duct tape. There is a place where you can peek through the rhododendron at the white meat of Second Ledge. It is a good place to scout your route. It isn't a bad place to reflect a bit. I stood at this place many times in the years I worked here, though I wasn't doing much reflecting then.

I sent close to three hundred kids over the horizon line here at Second Ledge, two to a boat. The kids were young criminals, aged thirteen to eighteen, not all of them urban and poor. They'd raped, stolen cars, sold crack, burned barns, and stabbed teachers. They'd done other things, too, like been caught and tried and found guilty and sentenced to the thirty-day, Outward Bound-adaptive adventure program where I worked.

When you do such work for a time, you try to keep your mouth shut about things like therapeutic value and other such marketing scams. Live in the woods for thirty days, six times a year, and such definitions grow absurd fast. All I know is the kids were wild. They were wild and I was right there with them.

So it was my line of work, a job that nobody likes to admit bears likeness to that of a being slave driver in prior eras. I won't waste your time with the obvious connections like on day one giving the kids backpacks in exchange for their cuffs and shackles, but I'll tell you this: I'm still haunted by the rap lyrics the kids spit in my face when I told them to put their lifejackets back on and get in the canoe and go over the falls. If you can't swim, the logic went, the lifejacket would swim for you.

If the kids didn't run Second Ledge, or if they refused repeatedly to hike or climb or clean the big pot or gather wood or bury their crap in a hole, then we sent them back to detention centers for six to nine months of foosball, cigarettes, push-ups, bad food, and medications. I didn't like to remove kids. I still believe that their being outside was the best thing going. It was important to me that these kids had the smell of good, rich woods and wild water and weather in their muscle memory, especially if they spent their remaining days in prison or other institutions, as many of them, in this country, in these times, do.

IT IS LIKE an arena below Second Ledge, house-sized boulders piled on the bank as it arcs with the river's bend, the stripped, water-dense logs a reminder of the Chattooga's rowdier moods. Below that bend, however, the river widens into a slower, more meditative groove for a mile or so until a rapid called Eye of the Needle. I run the sneak route there and pull out on the beach. I poke around a bit, notice an inordinate number of fallen pines. It looks like a microburst or tornado has slammed the slope. I sit on a boulder. I read, nap in the sun. Read some more. No other boaters appear. It is Saturday. Probably all the boaters are crowding Section Four, their adrenal glands the size of baseballs.

Lounging on the boulder, I finish James Salter's delicious novel, A Sport and a Pastime. A line near the end of that story sinks its barbs. "The more clearly one sees the world, the more one is obliged to pretend it does not exist." The sentence feels like a statement that sometimes feels true to me but now does not. "The more clearly one sees the world," it seems to me now, the harder I must work to make sense of what I see, of what's missing, what remains, and what could be. I'm glad that Salter's characters spark such reckoning. Such novels, like all great works of art, bolster my confidence in the human animal, suggest we have the imagination to take care of the last wild places, both on earth and in ourselves.

I DON'T BELIEVE it is too much to ask our state and federal governments to preserve the integrity of the entire Chattooga watershed. By protecting the river and other wild places like it, we are protecting nothing less than our very souls. Who doesn't want intact watersheds? Humanity's primal bias against wilderness, as well as the more recent bias against nostalgia, is boring. We want the threat and delight of deep, untrammeled woods, of the mysteries they contain—in their soil, their micro flora, their plants and animals and their rot. We crave rivers that run clean and pure, just as we crave the personal integrity that comes from preserving land for the sake of the land and all the non-human life that depends on intact woods and waterways.

Conservationists have been rallying for decades, but decades are nothing in the scheme of our deep past. The Anglo-Saxon sense of danger inherent in wilderness runs deep in us. We must act with the same energy with which we've butchered and continue to butcher wild places. In the American South, population and development is growing as dense as the woods used to be. Wilderness issues are linked to every social issue—sexism, racism, etcetera, all the isms, as well as poverty, justice, food. We have a gift for complicating these issues, but in the end it is a matter of character, respect, taking care. We will lose nothing by protecting the Chattooga watershed in its entirety. What we have to gain is immeasurable. If we really need another gated, second home development that greenwashes its resource-depleting existence by calling itself a preserve, why don't we build it along a river that's already been compromised? Can we not find lumber from those same woods? Better yet, use salvaged lumber, restore old homes, build with cob or old tires. Radical, maybe, but isn't it time to admit that what's considered radical—in all issues—is often not only simple, but simply makes sense.

People pay a lot of lip service to terms like wildness and wilderness. I don't like having to define either one. As far as I can tell, wildness is to wilderness as spirituality is to religion, but this is an analogy as thick and tangled as the rhododendron groves visible from the canoe, up there, here and there through the trees. Wild places, in the land and in our selves and in the souls of all life, tend toward balance. It is a balance that goes beyond science, rationality, and other efforts at explanation. It is a balance that just as often steers towards excess as towards poverty. Look at a river in flood. Look at trout gorging during a hatch, limbs hustling for sunlight. The kid cutting himself, the kid having a tennis lesson. The woods in blossom, the woods in drought.

So wildness and wilderness, being extensions of the same root, are linked in mysterious ways. Some claim that wildness is about acceptance, that it's a state of being, a constantly evolving way of tolerating things as they are, in all their duty and persistence, unknowableness and unseeability, tolerating them because human or not, they are natural. According to this way of thinking, the Chattooga could be sold tomorrow, maybe to Disney, and ground broken for a massive resort, and I should not lose one ounce of wildness in my soul. Such thinking says that resorts are just as wild as the river and all birds, beasts, and flowers that make their home here, because resorts are human dwellings and humans are animals and wild. It says, too, that I am nostalgic.

And yes I am nostalgic. Wildly so. I believe in this place. I believe in all pristine places, but especially in the Chattooga. It is a place dense and lush and dark and bright and loud with quiet. It contains more of the power I understand as God than any other place or institution or group of people I've known. But mostly I believe in it because it touches me deeply and because it touches others deeply and because they believe in it and take care of it the best they know how.

IT ISN'T UNUSUAL to drift among such thoughts on the river, especially in a canoe. Canoeing is not a distracting sport. It is more serious than fun, though paddlers take fun seriously. You have to. You have to escape and replenish sometimes in order to deal with these times. Being in a boat on moving water helps one to sort the mind's jetsam. When you look at the world from a canoe, what you see and feel suggests that we need not trust most of what we see and less of the thoughts we inherit and are taught to think. The hemlocks today are many shades of green and yellow, depending on their posture and the light and my relation to them. Where the river runs deep over sand it is so green as to verge on purple. At the rapids it turns white. At the shallows, depending on the bed—rock, sand, silt, or some combination—it is red, yellow, orange, and all or none of the above.

The moon is larger tonight. The sound of the river pulses through the fire's heat. The driftwood burns fast and hot. Above the fire a hemlock bough sways, the smoke filtering though its aphid-stressed needles. I am camped on the South Carolina-side of the Chattooga, between Thrift's Ferry and the Highway 76 bridge. It feels different making camp in the woods above the river. I like the change. Last night's sandbar experience combined with a long day on the water makes the woodland vantage a kind of relief, as though the river's voices were beginning to get to me.

The river's voices were getting to me long before last night. I think of the Chattooga every day. Mental snapshots, smells, sounds—it is loyalty, that's all. I feel it in every river or stream or puddle I cross, no matter how far from this magic ribbon tying Highlands to Tugaloo. As I drove to the river from North Central

North Carolina, it felt like salamanders were trying to crawl out of my skull and ribs. I mean it tickled and it hurt, a good hurt.

When I came to guide on the Chattooga in 1990, I was eighteen and felt like I was coming home. My upbringing in Atlanta was riddled with the polluted currents that ultimately undo a family. I was lucky that my father took me camping, canoeing, fishing, and hunting with him. On those trips, I saw a man transformed; a man haunted and graced by demons I'll never understand, the same demons that probably inhabit many veterans of the war in Vietnam, all wars, and that piggyback onto their children. On those trips I was so lucky to take, I felt a great weight fall from my father and me. We were alive in ways that seemed impossible at home.

I thrived in the wild quiet of the Chattooga. I loved the full-time, daily engagement with and faith in the elemental. The promise and indifference of the land's darkness and light, its bugs and birds, flowers and snakes, everything, felt as necessary as the crazy weather, the camaraderie of fellow river rats—the parties, the injuries, the sleep. Perhaps most of all, I enjoyed feeling the hearts of our customers opening—their voices quieter, their movements more reverent—as the river tossed our rafts like so many weird rubber bubbles.

Though I have moved a lot since then, and have inflicted my share of damage on places and people, the feeling has not changed. The degradation of the river of my youth—the Chattahoochee—like that of my family and the city of Atlanta where I was raised, is what it is for me—a source of reluctant acceptance. The Chattooga has never stopped being the place where I come closest to knowing clarity, which is, in a sense, being okay with the likely impossibility of it. Out here, without the onslaught of civilization, I can embrace the tough changes that need to happen, even if I can't make sense of them.

Junkies have camped here recently. The little blue caps of

their needles lay scattered around the fire ring. I gather and burn them, the stench of plastic vague but present. Better here to get high, I suppose, than some dank, mold-infested TV room or shit-hole alley. It is a milder night than the previous one. For dinner I knife chicken liver spread from a can onto bread and then heat more chicken and dumplings. Food goes down easy after a long day on the water.

As the meal settles, I remember the yellow violets and bluets that were in blossom near Eye of the Needle. There is no balm more soothing than late-winter wildflowers, their brightness among the still bare trees. I think of the wood ducks accelerating on wing from their roosts in the roots of the bank, of Norris Campbell, his shack that may or may not still stand in the woods above Three Roostertails. I stoke the fire. I watch it burn. And later, for a nightcap, I wander to the river's edge, watch the moonlight and the waves do their thing.

About the Book

The font, Electra, designed in 1935 by William Addison Dwiggins, has been a standard book typeface since its release because of its evenness of design and high legibility. In the specimen book for Electra, Dwiggins himself points out the type's identifying characteristics: "The weighted top serifs of the straight letters of the lower case: that is a thing that occurs when you are making formal letters with a pen, writing quickly. And the flat way the curves get away from the straight stems: that is a speed product." Electra is not only a fine text face but is equally responsive when set at display sizes, realizing Dwiggins' intent when he set about the design: "…if you don't get your type warm it will be just a smooth, commonplace, third-rate piece of good machine technique, no use at all for setting down warm human ideas, just a box full of rivets…. I'd like to make it warm, so full of blood and personality that it would jump at you."

Photographs of the Chattooga River
COVER: Bull Sluice
FIRST TITLE PAGE: Big Creek Falls
END PAGE: Second Ledge
Copyright © 1999, 2001 by Charles E. Zartman

Design by Robert B. Cumming, Jr.

Thorpe Moeckel has guided trips on rivers and trails throughout the Appalachians. His first book of poems, *Odd Botany*, won the Gerald Cable Award and was published in 2002. He teaches in the MFA Program at Hollins University and lives with his family on a small farm near the James River in Western Virginia.

Printed in the United States
204767BV00001BB/1/P

9 781604 542004